GUERRILLA THEATRE
FOR FAIRES AND FESTIVALS

By J. Paul Moore

For information or to order more copies of this handbook contact:
IonDrivePublishing.com

To contact the author:
JPaulMoore@MSN.Com

© Copyright J. Paul Moore, 2009
ISBN 978-0-9817143-7-0

All rights reserved. No portion of this material may be reproduced in any form or by any means without the written permission of the author; not no how, not no way.

Printed in the U.S.A.

ABOUT THE AUTHOR

A Theatre Arts major at Los Angeles City College, J. Paul Moore began a 35-year affiliation with the original Renaissance Pleasure Faire in 1967. Over his tenure, Mr. Moore has taught pre-faire workshops in Elizabethan Language, Swashbuckling 101, and Guerrilla Theatre. In addition to writing and directing many stage shows he has portrayed major theme characters: Robin Hood, Sir Francis Drake and the Lord Mayor, Captain Sir Tristan Hawkins. A co-founder of theatrical and environmental groups, J. Paul has also directed a covert band of theatre guerrillas, "The Lord Mayor's Players" for several faires.

Much of the material detailed in the *Compendium of Bits*, Chapter VI, evolved from the talents of these troupes.

Mr. Moore and his former wife Sandy are proud parents of three children Ryan, a boy and the oldest, Morgan and Courtney both girls. Ryan and Morgan grew up at the Renaissance Pleasure Faires and Courtney is a five-year veteran of The Colorado Renaissance Festival. Ryan and his wife Danielle have recently welcomed Mr. Moore's first grandson, Alexander, to the world.

A magician as well as an actor and author, J. Paul has also written, **Busking as a Mercenary Art or How to Hustle a Bar** and **Reserve Stock v.s.o.p.** both books on sleight-of-hand magic. For the world of swordplay and dering-do he has a handbook entitled **Swashbuckling 101** and is currently working on a project entitled **Archaeo/Mythology-Eire** which examines and compares both historical and legendary timelines of prehistoric Ireland.

ACKNOWLEDGEMENTS

To list, by name, the many people who have been invaluable in the compilation of this book would take another book in itself. Interspersed throughout the following material, however, I will drop a slew of names you never heard of. Some, perhaps, will ring loud bells. Many of the ideas here in have come from, or evolved through, the host of talented, creative people I have known at faires over the years. I am lucky to be a part of such a "family" and I thank them for being. That said, I do wish to give special thanks to my pal of several decades, Billy Scudder for being a beacon of positive light, and, to my friend and guide Merlin for dragging me into the world of the word processor, to Ms. Annie Lore for curing me of using *them* and *they* in the singular, and finally to my buddy Brennan for letting me crash on his couch .

Dedicated to
Phyllis Patterson and Ron Patterson

For

The
Renaissance
Pleasure Faire

Thank-you

FORWARD
By David Springhorn

There are humbling moments in life (my child's birth being the greatest) which befall one. To be asked to write the forward to one of your mentor's books is not small among them.

J. Paul Moore taught me more than "gorilla" theater. He gave me the gift of communicating Magick to an audience; how to alter their reality and my own; to destroy the thin membrane between actor and spectator; to put myself on the line so I could draw them into the faire's communal soul. Think I am laying it on too thick? Well, pal, if you're not having this same intense personal experience with the crowd, you ain't doin' it right!!!!!!

What we have here is a battle manual made by a Captain in the trenches and I highly suggest you follow it!!

Thank-you for this Book, J. Paul. It's about time you shared your secrets with us and stopped lavishing them only on the audience.

David Springhorn, Spiritual guide to cosmic foolishness

CONTENTS

PREFACE ---------- 1

I   THEATRE OF OPERATIONS ---------- 5

II   TOOLS OF THE TRADE -------------- 7

III   BASIC TRAINING -------------------- 12

IV   STYLES OF ATTACK ----------------- 19

V   BATTLE PLANS ---------------------- 25

VI   COMPENDIUM OF BITS -------------- 27

VII   RANDOM THOUGHTS --------------- 40

THE FINAL WORD --------------------- 44

AFTERWORD

PREFACE

WHAT IS GUERRILLA THEATRE?

Guerrilla Theatre is an interactive style of improvisational performance allowing audiences to become actual players in the show. The experience is by turns, aggressive, passive, intimate, distant, obvious and covert. There are as many approaches as there are people to approach it. It is a broad, colorful and captivating canvas.

Although a passion and/or talent for improvisation will prove invaluable in guerrilla theatre, distant visuals, and covert operations require little or no such calling. In fact, you can oft times recruit players from the audience to join your merry band on the

"Celts comin! Hide yer wimmin!"

spot – some more than others. As a lone wolf or member of a group you can create an exhilarating and compelling under-current of village life in Shakespeare's England.

Guerrilla Theatre is not, for the most part, meant to gather and hold a crowd. It moves through a moving audience, pauses occasionally, circles the wagons and disappears into the crowd itself. It is a nebulous energy infusing itself into the moment, exhorting a chuckle, planting information, stirring thought or, on occasion, eliciting a response from the audience.

You are the 'conversation overheard in passing' or 'the Town Crier' or perhaps an entire scene played on the move, through the crowd, against the grain. (Okay, perhaps I am getting ahead of myself.) It is relating to the audience response from within your character that offers the challenge to your improvisational skills. Sometimes you will be brilliant. Other times…

SPEAKING OF THEATRE

Because it is performed on the move, in the crowd, to a non-captive audience, the discipline for guerrilla theatre must be even more intense than in the traditional enclosed proscenium style of theatre. Your voice must be strong and articulate, your body language definite and your audience awareness keen. <u>Theatre must communicate</u>. If the audience goes away not knowing what you were doing then you may as well not have done it. Time after time I see players furiously acting away, tearing their passion to tatters while the audience streams by, oblivious to their efforts.

In the words of Mr. Jerry Blunt, author of <u>The Composite Art of Acting</u> and head of the Los Angeles City College Theatre Arts Department when I attended in the 60's: *Theatre must be Definite, Dynamic, Economic and Telling.* Theatre is not real life. Theatre picks and chooses those things which further the story, and deletes those which detract from it. Theatre is illusion. The better your choices, the more complete the illusion. You must remain aware of controlling the center of interest and supporting your fellow players. The best theatre is ensemble theatre. Just because you <u>can</u> dominate a scene is no reason why you should!!!

Auditioning for Shakespeare – "Where the bee sucks…"

PRIME OBJECTIVE

The purpose of this weighty tome is to guide you and your troupe through a specific technical orientation of guerrilla theatre, set out some individual and collective exercises to get you up off your butt and doing something, and hopefully, to spark your own imagination to create a living environment.

So dive in. I suggest you keep this book in the bathroom so when you have a chance to *'get away'* from time to time, you can peruse the offerings, extracting some applicable tid-bit with each visit.

Shamus cons a farmer out of his money

As the bathroom may be cramped when working with a group, perhaps you could take the group to a park. The more you work together, of course, the more comfortable you will become as an improvisational squad, company or battalion. One idea sparks another and before you know it you have an end-product amazingly evolved from what, at first, may have seemed like a simple idea. Have fun. <u>The idea is to have fun.</u>

I. THEATRE OF OPERATIONS

It is my guess that the appeal of this handbook will be to people involved with one or more of the hundreds of theme fairs around the country. As the great majority of these are Olde English oriented, I shall draw my references from my home shire, *"Chipping Under Oakwood";* the original Renaissance Pleasure Faire of Southern and Northern California. These techniques and styles are easily adapted to other themes.

Your audience is a moving target of fluctuating intensity. To understand the nature of the beast, let us follow a few scenarios to plot its movement through the faire:

1. The audience gathers at the front gate prior to opening. Most likely they are there treated to some sort of opening bally and should be in a cheery mood by the time the gates open. They will enter in a rush. You might have greeters or Mongers (theatrical street sellers) just inside the gate to keep the energy building. Let them come in and get their bearings for the first hundred yards or so. Scope out the terrain; which way does the crowd travel? Get upstream and work your way downstream through the oncoming crowd.

2. Look for gathering places. Ale Stands, food courts, ATM lines, privy banks. Here you have a semi-stationary crowd. You must play the crowd without keeping them from their ale, turkey leg or macramé flower pot holder.

3. Remember that the ticket lines out front continue after the morning rush has entered. Many events have a second and third rush. Get them off to a good start. Work the lines.

4. Moving into the afternoon, the crowd begins to meander. Look for people you "set up" earlier in the day. Instill anticipation of things to come. *"The Queen comes upon us within the hour." "I hear the King is abroad".*

5. As parades go by, blend into the crowd and disseminate information. *"Irish mercenaries, you know. "Oh look! There be the Lord Sheriff ...sober!"* If it is the King or Queen get the crowd involved. Get them to remove their hats and shout *"God save the whosit."*

6. As the day begins to wind down, people start making their way toward the exit. This is a grand opportunity to leave them with one of those memorable last impressions you dreamed up during workshops.

Here then, are half a dozen obvious theatres of operation. Of course you can work the booths themselves but you must be sensitive to the needs of the vendors. They have time and money invested in their booth and will not appreciate you blowing off their customers. Be aware!

II. TOOLS OF THE TRADE

Commitment to the experience is clearly the most valuable tool at your disposal. Put on your, mask, literal or figurative, and get into the fray. Experiment. Try things. Keep the things that work and drop the things that do not. The only way to fail is to not try. If you are doing a bit and it is dieing, make an exit, go off behind a booth, have a 7UP or something and discuss why it didn't work, regroup and go try it again on a different audience. At some point you will either hone that improv into a finely-tuned piece of quintessential theatre or flush it as a "noble experience" best laid away for future war stories. *("Remember the time.....")* Sometimes your best choice is to run for your life.

AN ASIDE

In the early 70's at RPF-South, Billy Scudder, Judy Kory, Barton Jay, "Que" and I were being directed by Ken E. Milliken in a play in progress he was writing called <u>The Prince of Curd</u> or something like that (there were a lot of cheese jokes). Ken E. never did get around to finishing the script and was guiding us via improv onstage. Unfortunately, Kenny was the only one who had any idea what the story was and even though we players were chewing up the scenery the show was going nowhere. I spotted Sean, the young man who was playing Robin Hood that year, watching from a nearby tree. After making an exit, I sidled over to him, procured some arrows and told him to mime shooting us all dead. Slipping backstage again I distributed the arrows among the cast. We then each went out and executed individual death-by-arrow scenes. When we lay in a heap on the stage, the audience broke in to applause, at which time we hopped up, took a bow and ran for our lives. (Sometimes the dragon wins).

Of course, your body and voice are major tools. Surely you don't need this book to tell you to do voice and body warm-ups before going out to play. It does not really matter <u>which</u> exercises you do as long as you do <u>some</u>. My focus, when we get there, will be to present some exercises for tuning in to one another, building trust and fostering confidence.

Costumes and props are also great booby traps and attention getters. Keep your eye out for interesting props. Take, say, a three handled whatsit and pass it around the circle, having each person relate to it in a different way. Entire scenes are known to take form around a single prop.

VERILY, ANOTHER ASIDE

I thought it would be a funny premise to have someone out in the crowd for the purpose of putting up a sign even though being unable to read. He/she would take signs out of a bag and ask the patrons what they said. Props gave me a burlap bag with a bunch of small

signs saying such things as *Post no Bills, One Way, No Way, Sheep Crossing, This Way, That Way* and the like. The bit worked well. Then Judy took the *This Way* and *That Way* signs and stood at the crossroad. Holding *This Way* in one hand and *That Way* in the other and saying not a word, she got a laugh and a good deal of indecisive reaction from everyone who passed by. Then we noticed there were a lot of *Way's* so Carl made up a few more signs and we wound our Wayfarer Parade through the Faire, in single file with each of us separated by about 15 seconds. By the end of the run we had grown to a procession of 20 people: *This Way, That Way, Both Ways, No Way, All the Way, The Family Way, One Way, Another Way,*

The True Way, My Way, The Highway, Curds and Whey, etc. and of course bringing up the rear was a player in chains carrying a sign that said *Burma Slave*, just for the over fifty crowd who remember the old Burma Shave signs. Our parade was a great success and I am flattered to hear that this parade idea and several others have popped up at faires around the country. I relate this story as an example of how a simple premise can evolve into a totally different and effective bit.

The same holds true with costumes. Pool a bunch of costume pieces, put them together in different ways and hit the streets for five minutes. You will discover great things. I put together a god-awful Santa wig with an even worse beard, headband and tattered robe. Holding a lantern on high I went out as Diogenes, looking for an honest man. I would approach someone as though I had finally found what I was looking for, only to realize my mistake and turn away muttering *"No... no..."* I was pleasantly surprised to see how many people recognized the character and jumped in with things like *"You got the wrong guy there,"* and *"Oh no, not him".* The whole thing grew out of playing around with costume pieces and props.

And don't forget about the terrain. Hillsides, bridges, trees, booths, big rocks. **Paramount to all is your own imagination.** Let it soar. This is no time for restrictions. You are among friends. They are all in your movie and you are in theirs. The more you work, relate, rehearse and communicate with one another the stronger a unit you will become. Soon you will establish a solid ensemble. You should be having fun by now.

THE LORD MAYOR'S PLAYERS' WAYFARER'S PARADE

Renaissance Pleasure Faire - South

III. BASIC TRAINING

It is difficult to rehearse audience inter-active theatre without the audience. What you can do, however, is get together the nuts and bolts and establish scenarios and outlines. You can learn who your fellow players are and build a co-operative, creative atmosphere. I'm assuming that you're a troupe of around a dozen players. If you're a large group of twenty, thirty or more, divide up into more workable sized groups. This is not to say that you will not all work together as a large group on occasion but smaller ones are better for working out bits and afford more opportunity for individual participation.

THE PROGRAM

HAVE A PARTY. Pool some resources and have a party for the troupe at someone's house. Rent a couple of videos that are somehow related to what you want to do as a troupe. High comedy, low comedy, authenticity, realism, intrigue, fantasy. You name it, your video store has it. I do not mean to suggest that you should imitate these movies. No matter how well you imitate Monty Python, you are still <u>imitating</u> Monty Python. The movies are meant to establish a mood, a focus and create a common denominator. Do not expect to accomplish anything in particular at the party. Its purpose is merely to bring everyone together. Before the end of the party set the date, place and time for your first rehearsal.

FIRST REHEARSAL

Quite likely someone has emerged as the group director. If it is you, remember that the idea is to direct not dictate. Gather the group in a circle and try some of the following suggestions. Also be open to suggestions from the group. After all, you are working together!

Gather your group in a circle and do some warm-up and improvisation exercises.

1. Have someone in the circle lead in physical warm up exercises.

2. Have someone else take over to do vocal warm-ups.

3. Go around the circle having the players introduce themselves. If you have a small group of old friends this will be superfluous, but if you're a sizable company most likely you don't know every name and it will take some time to know everyone. (No one wants to admit to not remembering your name so don't rule out the idea of wearing nametags for a while.)

IMPROVISATION EXERCISES

1. **Passing the Clap.** I got the clap from the immortal Sandra Mehterian, once Mistress of Mongers. This is a good exercise for turning individual focus into group focus. Standing in your circle, one person starts by turning to the left and clapping hands. The next person to the left then turns to the left and claps. Continue to pass the clap around the circle, varying the speed, intensity and attitude. Someone can reverse the direction by double clapping.

2. **Throwing energy.** This can be done with a volleyball, beach ball, tennis ball or imaginary energy ball. (I think the imaginary ball works best because it will do what ever you want it to do.) Again, in the circle, one person throws the ball to someone else in the circle. As they do they make some sort of sound: *"Whoosh... Zing... Bumpeta, bump."*

The receiver catches the ball, repeats the sound and then throws the ball to someone else, making a new sound. Keep it going. Get creative with the sounds. Vary the intensity, speed, etc.

3. **Walk like an Egyptian.** Begin to walk in a circle. Have someone call out adjectives and/or descriptions. Everyone continues to walk in that way. ie: Happy, tired, anxious, wary, old man, young girl, royalty, peasant, etc.

4. **Prop talk.** As mentioned earlier, pass props around the circle having everyone relate to them differently.

5. **Story, story.** Someone in the circle starts to tell a story. After getting a minute or so into the story the person indicates someone else in the circle who must immediately pick up and carry on the story line then pass it off to another player. Continue in this fashion.

6. **This is a what?** This one comes through Billy Scudder and is rumored to have actually started in Never-never-land. It is fun, silly, stimulating and challenging. Still in your circle, the starting person turns to the left and hands the next person an object. (It can be anything. Let's say it's an apple.) The starter says, *"This is an apple."* The next person, before taking the apple says, *"A what?"* The first person, repeats *"An*

apple." The second person, taking the apple says, *"Oh, an apple."* The second person now turns to the left, offers the apple saying, *"This is an apple."* The third person, before taking the apple says, *"A what?"* The second person turns back to the first person and says, *"A what?"* The first person says, *"An apple."* The second person turns to the third person saying *"An apple".* The third person says, *"Oh, an apple."* Follow this pattern as the apple makes its way around the circle.

Now for the fun and challenging part. While the apple is going around to the left, the starter begins the same routine to the right with an orange. *"This is an orange." "A what?" "An orange." "Oh, an orange."* This continues around the circle to the right. It takes a good deal of concentration to keep track of what is going on, especially when the items cross at the far end of the circle and continue their progress.

7. Building a machine. A classic improvisational exercise (that means it's old). A person goes to the center of the circle and begins some sort of a movement – let's say swinging one arm right and left. That action is kept going as another person enters the circle and adds a motion to the machine, and then another and so on until the entire troop is involved with the machine. If you want to push the envelope, make the machine have some specific end purpose. It plucks chickens, pours beer, whatever.

8. What am I doing? I have that consummate fool Michael Schaffer to thank for this one. One person begins to play some sort of action. ie: Change the oil on a car, tune a piano, scrub the floor. As the players in the circle begin to realize what the person is doing, they join in the action by doing something that adds to the scene. ie: Clean the windshield, polish the piano lid, sweep the floor... Continue until everyone is involved.

9. Powering up. I find this to be very valuable for binding everyone's energy and focus to the task at hand. Just before you're ready to go on, form a tight circle with every person's hand touching. Each person begins to emit a low tone. The tone begins to grow in intensity. As the tone grows, the hands begin to vibrate and slowly rise, en masse. The whole thing builds to a crescendo as the hands erupt into the air with a great cry of sound. Very stimulating and bonds the players to a common focus.

These, then, are some "basic training" exercises to get you started. If you have others you like better by all means use them. The idea is to build a supportive atmosphere of trust and creative freedom.

REHEARSING ROUTINES

Now that you have warmed up, pick a routine, cast it and try it out with the rest of the company pretending to be faire-goers. Re-cast and try it again. Keep doing this until everyone has a chance to try it. Discuss what you've discovered.

Pick another routine and work it the same way. Keep trying different bits. Ideas for new bits will emerge. Try them, work with them; some will be brilliant and will evolve into great scenarios. Some will suck. The only way to know is to try them out, revise and re-try.

GAFFER APPELWRIGHT. One of the truly great street acts

IV. STYLES OF ATTACK

1. Personal contact, one on one. You make contact with a patron and elicit a response. Perhaps you ask them a question: *"Hast thou seen my Wife's goose?"* Give a person something to hold as in the Apple Bit where you ask someone to hold a basket of apples and say you you'll be right back. You leave and Goodwife Datchett comes along with a Constable looking for her stolen apples. They spot the guest holding the apples and merriment ensues. The guests friends will jump in and you will have set up a target for later. Anytime you encounter this person, you need only wag your finger to get a reaction.

2. The Town Crier. Stand up and read off some of your best material. You could announce coming shows, rewards for cutpurses, lost and found; and my personal favorite, "A Look at the News" which is a braiding of contemporary news with olde English interpretation and satirical parody.

As an example, when San Francisco had a bicyclist uprising called **Critical Mass,** we interpreted it as an outbreak of Hobby Horse riders dubbed **Critical Mess**. Tom made up some stick horses and we rode around blocking traffic and demanding more trails for hobby horses. When finally busted by the Constable (one of our players) we hoisted the hobby horse rear ends, dropped little wooden blocks and rode away.

THE LORD MAYOR'S PLAYERS - RPF-N / Hobby Horse protest "Critical Mess"

In the 70's when there was a gasoline shortage and rationing, we had a Hay Shortage. Dark horses could get hay on Monday, Wednesday; light horses could get hay on Tuesday and Thursday. Dapple-grays were to be considered "odd" horses.

YET ANOTHER ASIDE

Just a quick caveat about contemporary parallels: This must be done with a lighthearted, tongue-in-cheek attitude. Do not lose track of the fact that you are presenting escapist theatre to take people out of their everyday world. No one wants to be beaten over the head with man's inhumanity to man. A <u>little</u> awareness goes a long way.

3. Overheard conversation. Set it up so that the patron overhears this in passing. The scene could involve two characters, from something Shakespearean, strolling through the crowd playing the scene as though there were hidden cameras in the trees and all these people were extras. Perhaps a couple of ladies walking along gossiping. *"Disgraceful...The Lord Sheriff and the Miller's daughter...in the barn!"* or disseminating information. *"The Queen will be here within the hour."* Use this technique on a massive scale to infuse the audience with an undercurrent of shire life.

4. Parades and moving masses. Full-on parades fall under an entirely different heading, worthy of its own book. They require extensive organization, routing and pacing. Small, non-threatening processions such as the aforementioned Wayfarers Parade or the Hobby Horse Prance, however, can work well for you and the show. Moving masses could be a bunch of happy singing sailors making their way from one Ale stand to another. Perhaps a gaggle of Aldermen making a fuss over the Queen's eminent arrival.

5. Distant Visuals. A Unicorn on the hillside; a duel in the distance; an armored knight riding through the trees; a Satyr in the bushes. A flight of Faeries disappearing around the corner. Jack of the Green slipping through the mustard weeds - things to be glimpsed far off.

Distant Visuals pique the imagination. Father Charlatanus arrives.

6. Disembodied voices. Many events have burlap walls and view-cuts. The audience can hear through these walls. Why not give them something to hear? Hot gossip about the Queen and the Earl of Essex; intrigue at court; an old Danny Kaye routine.

7. The captive audience. Any and all lines, from the ticket booths to the privies. These folks aren't going anywhere and will welcome some entertaining interplay. Perhaps approach people as they're washing their hands with, *"What! Will these hands ne'er be clean?"*

They may or may not know it's from Macbeth. A little privy humor goes a long way.

8. Street Theatre. Differs from Guerrilla Theatre in that it is more permanent. Whereas Guerrilla Theatre is hit and run, Street Theatre grabs and holds attention long enough to play out a more lengthy script.

THE GREENWOOD PLAYERS RPF-1971

ROBIN HOOD Street Theatre

V. BATTLE PLANS

Size up the area you will be influencing. Is it all the faire, just a section, or within a structure of some sort? How many of you are there? Let us say we are a troop of a dozen players and we are working the front area of the faire.

Looking around, we note that the opening rush will be coming this way, over there is the first chance to get something to drink and over there people will be standing around waiting for their friends to get out of the privy. Here is an area where they will be shopping and here we get to a stage.

Decide which scenarios will fit each area. Over by the Ale-stand we'll do Pregnant Molly and The Love Letter. Let's run the Pig Bit against the flow from the stage to the front entrance. We can put a pair of faeries and a Satyr off there in the bushes. Put someone over there by the Privies, leave the shopping area clear and let's put a Town Crier by the stage with news and announcements of coming acts. Assign the players, run over it a couple of times and lie in wait for the unsuspecting audience.

The crowd you are playing to is on the move. **Wait about ten minutes and do the same bits all over again to a new audience.** Work these bits for an hour or two from opening on and you will have played to the first several thousand people, getting them off to a good start. You have broken the ice and let the folks know it is okay to play.

Set up another battle plan for the closing two hours and you afford yourself the opportunity to be the parting image. Naturally it should be a positive image, with a sub-text of *"Thank-you for shopping Wal-Mart. Y'all come back now."*

As for the rest of the day, follow the formula. Size up the areas and throw in some bits. See how it works, expand and modify. Keep track of what works and what doesn't so that when you get together over tea at the end of the day you can compare notes.

You should have morning warm-ups to set up the *Modus Dejour* and evening meetings to review the gleanings of the day. Having coffee and muffins available in the morning, perhaps some cold drinks through the day and something afterward will go a long way toward raising *espirit de corps* among your undoubtedly over-worked troops.

THE LORD MAYOR'S PLAYERS - RPF-S -1999

VI. COMPENDIUM OF BITS

Of course it is expected that your own commitment will create new and exciting material. I include this compendium only to help give you a jumping-off place. Certainly you may use any of the enclosed material just as written, however it is obviously old material and hardly worthy of the creative genius that wells within you and yours.

A few words of credit to the sources of the enclosed material. Very few of the following ideas are original with me. Most of them either came from the many talented people I have had the honor of working with over the decades or have evolved out of the same sort of group efforts that will create your own unique direction.

ARSENAL:
TECHNIQUES AND GIMMICKS

The Quick Shot - For use on the move. Basically one-liners to be said in passing, perhaps getting some eye contact and, blessed be, a response. These can be directed toward an individual or to the crowd of a general area; Things such as: **Passing an Ale Stand,** *"Don't just stand there! For God's sake drink something."* **About a man with a dog,** *"Fresh meat! Dog, on the paw."*

Irish parade coming, *"Celts comin, hide yer wimmen!"* (Let someone else do the sheep jokes, PLEASE) **To a man with a slung camera,** *"Wearing your Cod Piece a bit high there M'Lord?"* **To a person perusing a map,** *"Fold the map up neatly, madam, tuck it away and get lost."* **To a man with a woman,** *"Ah, you found one ...and a pretty one too. Well done."* **To a woman with a man,** *"Have a care of him madam, he is well known in these parts."* **To a couple with a baby,** *"Ah, you bought one of the pretty ones. Did you get a good price?"* **or** *"Baby for sale, strong man child, good worker!"* You could even pause awhile and try to auction off the child, ending with something like, *"I'd hold out for a better price if I were you."*

AND YET ANOTHER ASIDE

A word or seventy about working to children. Some children frighten easily, particularly small children under five years old. It is best to play to the parents or older kids and let the curiosity of the younger ones pull them into the goings-on. If you sense a kid is about to go ballistic, exit. Leave them alone. You will only frighten them more by trying to smooth things over.

As you can see there are as many of these quick shots as you have time and patience to make up. The idea is to get the patron to smile, chuckle, laugh or roll on the ground in uncontrollable glee. The effectiveness of this is cumulative. No one bit does the job on its own. It's a tickle here, a giggle there, and a reaction over there that finally begins to manifest the illusion of a living environment. Although I tend to stress comedy, the same techniques can be used for furthering a more serious or even dramatic story line. What undercurrent of village life do you want to convey.

The Tape Loop - As the name implies this is like a continuous loop of tape that repeats itself over and over as you move through the crowd. The traveler hears it as a passing conversation or perhaps a brief interplay between themselves and a character. i.e.: Two fellows walking along. One says to the other, *"So I said, you draw steel on me and I'll have your guts for garters!"* 2nd fellow, *"Then what happened?"* 1st fellow, *"She apologized."* 2nd fellow, *"You always were a terror, Will'um."*

By this time you are passing out of the earshot of the people who heard this dialogue. Wait a few seconds and you can start the same routine all over again for a new audience. Continue to repeat the routine until you tire of it and are ready to move on to something else.

Let your imagination run rampant and you will come up with all kinds of dialogue that will work. Want something a little more classical? How about King Lear walking along talking to his Fool? Juliet with her nurse? Hamlet and Horatio? Falstaff and Hal? Ad infinitum. The more you do it the more ideas will come and the more you will refine the technique. Do not look around to see if anyone is reacting. Keep on the move. They hear it. The more often they encounter this energy the more interesting and realistic becomes the environment.

Interactive improvisation - Take a rehearsed premise into a selected area of the faire and improvise off the reactions of the audience.

Working against the grain - In most outdoor free-flow events there are certain traffic patterns throughout the day. The incoming and the exiting crowds. Large crowds leaving a big show. When possible, work against the flow of the crowd. If you go with the flow you are not constantly moving into a new audience. By moving into and through the audience flow you can play to a very large crowd in a very short time. (Perhaps I belabor the point).

Environmental areas – A group with a specific theme: Peasants, Royals, Pirates, Celts; create an area specific to their focus. This can be nothing more than a break area where the players have lunch in character or it can be an inclusive, hands-on environment where the patron is encouraged to participate. It is an environment where you have control of all aspects: costumes, language, and props. Sort of like a living painting.

The Council of "Sea Dog" Captains discussing the voyage of The Tainted Ladye

ROUTINES
THE ROYAL ESCORT

A scenario for a team of four: two trumpeters, one crier with a bell and one talker. They rush up to a patron. The talker is apologizing to the patron: *"Oh I most humbly beg your pardon for being late Sire."* (Aside to the Crier) *"The Earl of...I mean the Duke of...Oh what is your name M'Lord? Jones. Yes, of course, Jones"* (to the Crier) *"The Earl of Jones."* The Crier cues the trumpeters who blare forth, being careful where they blare. The Crier begins, *"Make way for the Earl of Jones!"* and they process down the road. Meanwhile the talker is fawning over the "Earl" with lavish praise and direction. *"Wave to the peasants M'Lord, they do love it so."* Escort him for 30 or 40 feet, wish them well and send them on their way. Hotfoot it back to pick up another unsuspecting patron. A nice alternative ending is to have a fifth player come up to the procession declaiming, *"This is not the Earl of Mumbly. I told thee to escort the Earl of Mumbly!"* He chases you off to find Mumbly whilst he apologizes profusely to the Earl of Jones.

ROMEO AND JULIET

For the more serious-minded, how about the opening street brawl scene, complete with real or hobbyhorses. Although more elaborate than our usual fare, this scene lends itself well to street pageantry for a selected area with sufficient crowd control.

HUE AND CRY

Several irate citizens chasing a fleeing Mountebank. *"That swill killed my cow!!"*...."*Call out the Constable!"*... *"Fetch a rope!!"* The Mountebank tries to hide in the crowd; tries to get patrons to help hide him; Citizens ask patrons for help. Play it as it flows.

WANNA BUY A PIG?

One of my personal favorite routines, this is a prime example of how a simple scenario can evolve into a full-fledged playlet with a beginning, middle, end ... and encore. This is also an excellent routine to be played against the grain of a moving audience.

A man goes through the crowd looking for his lost pig. *"Here pig, pig, pig...Have you seen my pig? Her name is Fanny. Here Fanny, here pig, pig, pig, sooooeeeeeeeeee!"* Scarcely thirty seconds after he has moved on, his wife comes along bewailing the loss of their pig.*"* About thirty seconds later a furtive, disreputable fellow with a

Pig for sale! Sell you the pig and the poke for a shilling."

lumpy sack sneaks through the crowd... *"Pig for sale... psssst, wanna buy a pig? Make you a good price. Sell you the pig AND the poke for only a shilling. Sweet succulent pig for sale!"*

When you get to the end of the play route the farmer and his wife spot the thief and chase him back through the crowd with... *"Stop that thief!" "I never stole no pig!"*... *"You pinched my Fanny! "*... *."I bought this pig from Tom, the Piper's son!"*...etc. until you have chased yourselves to a proper exit where you can fall out and tell each other the great things that happened to you on the route.

A FINAL ASIDE

I was playing the thief one time when a young lady, about twelve years old, wanted to know what a shilling was. I explained that it was a silver coin. She got a quarter from her father and wanted to buy my "pig in a poke". The only thing in the burlap bag was more burlap rolled up so I decided, 'What the heck' and I gave her the bag, snatched her quarter and dashed off in to the crowd. I watched from afar as she slowly opened the bag, took out the burlap, unrolled it and found nothing. About that time I, very obviously, tried to sneak past her. She spotted me and chased me down the road demanding her shilling back. It was the highlight of the day for me and I am sure she and her family will remember it for a while as well. Also the experience may well prepare the young lady for real world con artists.

LITTLE MISS PREGNANT

I am pretty sure this routine sprang, full blown, from the mind of the legendary Judy Kory who has helped shape RPF entertainment from the beginning. This is good to do near an Ale stand for the people standing around drinking. Also good for ticket lines and other captive audiences. A demure and obviously pregnant young girl sidles up to a guest with a shy ...*"Remember me?"* Whilst playing this bit they are approached by the biggest, baddest guy you can find to play her brother. He glares at the patron and drawls: *"Is this the one Molly? You just say the word Molly."* After a proper pause Molly says, *"No Tom, t'isnt."* She drifts away to find another victim, followed by Tom. Again this is a good set-up for playing later in the day.

CLASSIC SCENES

These are for those who are dedicated to re-creating an authentic, literary, Elizabethan atmosphere and they work "excellent-well". Lift short two or three-person scenes from various period authors. Shakespeare, Jonson, Marlow, Greene, etc. and perform them as you move through the crowd. The audience may never know what play the scenes are from. They will, however, overhear period conversations all around them adding to the Renaissance texture of the tapestry.

THE LOVE LETTER

Another good one for the standing-around crowd. A charming young girl, a-flush with the glow of new love, approaches a patron and requests help. She has a letter from her lover in the town but she cannot read. *"Wouldst thou read it for me?"* and she hands the letter to the patron. The letter very quickly turns out to be a letter of rejection. What kind of rejection, is up to you. Is it: *"Dearest Prudence, I regret that I will be unable to see thee again."* or is it *"Leave me alone! I never did love thee and thy breath smells like old cheese."* Whatever the approach, your letter should allow the actor to run the emotional gamut from rapture to doubt, disbelief, despair, anger, and vengeance with all the verbalizations to match.

A lovely variation on this idea, contributed by Phyllis Patterson, is to have the lady be Anne Hathaway. The letter is from her estranged husband, William Shakespeare who has abandoned the family to become an actor and playwright in London. Is he coming home? Does he miss the children? Is he sending money? It is, of course, helpful to have the letter written in <u>readable</u> olde English script on a parchment or rag type paper.

CHILD CARE

I have Dennis Green, a brilliant, creative player, to thank for this bit with which I have had great fun over several faires. Looking grubby, disheveled and somewhat threatening, a hulking ruffian slowly makes his way through the crowd carrying a large cudgel over his shoulder. Occasionally he hawks: *"CHILD CARE! Take care of the little un's for ya... Keep em quiet, I will... still as mice... Make em smart! quick-like, too... CHILD CARE!"* You will be amazed at the reactions. Play with them. (re-read the section on playing to children.)

LECHER IN CHAINS

Another Green bit. A lecher is dragged through the crowd on his way to the stocks. He is very unrepentant.

"I did it and I'm glad. I'd do it again. How about you, sweet'un?" Custodian keeps pulling him away from the women and on through the crowd.

MAKE A WISH

This bit I found to be wonderfully effective toward the end of the day. Costume a wizard type character and put him in the road near the main exit, giving out wishes. *"Wishes, they're free you know. Make a wish before you go."* Let people come up, gaze into a crystal and make a secret wish. When they are finished say something to the effect of *"So may it be... May your wish come true."* Sometimes a nice tag line, depending on the wisher, can be: *"I'm not sure where you are going to keep a pony, but that is your affair."*

"Gaze into the crystal and make a wish."

THE MAGIC SWORD

Another good bit to be done by the wizard. Look for children who have purchased one of the wooden swords sold at so many faires. Have him/her touch the sword to your crystal and think of a good thought. While this goes on, wave your hand and say something magical such as: *"Infuse this sword with magic light; may it only be used for the right."* The kid will be happy, the parents will be thrilled and if the guy who sells the swords sees you he may buy you a cottage in the country. Then again, maybe not. A good, selectively used, tag line: *"You are now invincible... Be careful where you test that out."*

Here, then, are some ideas to get you started. As your own focus narrows in on this style of performance you will become a veritable fountain of ideas. Pursue them all. Work through them with your troupe; expand, edit and sharpen them to performance level. Then trot them out to the public. Try your routines in the streets with the patrons then put them back in rehearsal mode and fine tune them some more.

VII. RANDOM THOUGHTS

Listen to your audience. Many great lines can come from them. Some are truly literate, talented people. Give them focus, let <u>them</u> be great! They will be thrilled to have played a part.

There is great material to be found in topical links. Translate present events into the period you are playing

Is it an election year? Perhaps the Lord Mayor is up for re-appointment and is being challenged by someone. Remember the idea is to be entertaining and take people into another time and place for an adventure. Preaching about a modern cause in contemporary language will not be as effective as lighter, more clever period humor. Political satire is one thing; beating a dead horse is something else.

Pace yourself through the day. Most events run for a good eight hours. Many are in extremely hot weather. While there may be a few who can run full-tilt all day long, most of us would be face-down in the dust long before our guests have toddled off into the parking lot. Certainly you are the only one who can set your schedule, but remember to leave plenty of time for rest, food and liquid.

Touching on this matter of liquids. **Water is your best friend!** Sodas are tasty but the sugar rush will work against you in the long run. Sugar dehydrates!

Establish a hooch,--a staging area, a secure, out of view, area somewhere in the faire where you can retreat to change costumes, store your belongings, or kick back and recover with a cup of tea.

EAT! Did I mention nourishment? You need fuel. It is easy to get caught up in the battle and not get around to eating. Here in the calm moment of reading this book, I ask you: Does that seem like a good idea? I think not.

Stay in character. Some patrons will try to break you. *"Yeah, but who are you really. What do you do in real life? Do you live around here?"* Even so, they will be disappointed if you break character. Answer their questions in character and they will get a kick out of it. *"I know not M'Lord, what be a T.V.?"* or *"did you tell me you had a vision?"..."Oh, I know, M'Lady, an inner-net is the one closest to the boat when I do go a-fishing..."* Some people will come up with incredible explanations of 21st century wonders. Let them. In the end you can pretend to be convinced that they must be insane, or witches or just funny.

In Elizabethan England women are subservient to men. They are possessions and have no public say in matters of state. Do you have any idea what kind of a debate can ensue when your character suggests that it is a waste of time to teach women to read or that they are best left to the home fires? It can get quite lively. Of course there will be some who just cannot take a joke. You know about them. Nevertheless, during that period a woman <u>ruled</u> England for forty-five years!

Twenty-first-century folk are television oriented. They sit. They watch. They say nothing. They only react when the laugh track tells them to. Part of your job is to get them to understand that your style of entertainment is interactive. Encourage them to say something, anything. Ask them questions. Have them hold things. Make eye contact. Theme fairs are a unique style of entertainment. Nowhere else can the audience interact with the players. Not television, not theatre, movies nor even theme parks like Disneyland. Once you get the patrons to understand that it is okay to play, great fun can be had by all..

On rare occasion you will encounter someone who just does not want to play. These are the terminally hip. Leave them alone and move on.

The importance of being earnest is not only a good title for a play but also indispensable advice for creating the overall experience of your event. Although I have put the accent on Elizabethan England, your event may be any theme. You will be well served to keep your language, props, costumes and routines true to the period you are re-creating.

Let us not conclude without touching on the pesky subject of *Thee* and *Thou*. Technically and accurately you would not address anyone of a higher station than yourself with thee or thou. Here is where I conflict historical theatre with theatrical history. It is my belief that the liberal (and, yes, inaccurate) use of *thee* and *thou* immediately imparts an Elizabethan flavor to the event. Additionally it is easily and readily done by anyone, without a knowledge of Elizabethan language. If you are a purist, by all means use the terms properly and gently pass on the proper usage to your fellow players but do not become enraged with any misuse when you encounter it being used to address a patron.

Making all the patrons M'Lords and M'Ladys is also not accurate but it adds immediately to the flavor of the event. It seems an easy price to pay for the effect achieved. You, of course, will decide the issue for yourself.

THE FINAL WORD

You hold in your hand an invitation and guide map to an exciting style of theatre that separates the theme fair from the theme swap meet. I hope I have clearly defined what Guerrilla Theatre is and how unique is its interactive format. Build your own troupe and be limited only by your own commitment, enthusiasm and budget.

I have laid out examples of scenarios which you may either adapt to your own needs or use to spark your own creativity. Finally, I hope I have instilled some inspiring concepts which will to help fine-tune your endeavor. It is my hope that this book will help establish Guerrilla Theatre as an entertainment style at the hundreds of themed events across the country. Have fun. <u>Are we having fun yet?</u>

All's well that ends well,

J. Paul Moore

AFTERWORD

I would like to thank Phyllis Patterson, the inventor of the Renaissance Faire experience in America, for her invaluable guidance in the editing of this handbook.

Her encouragement and spiritual support evolved a theatrical/historical venue that has flourished from coast to coast with a true renaissance of personal artistry and craftsmanship.